# Transforming Teaching Strategies

*Ensuring the Success of Kids These Days*

**Mary Endres Thomas**

Printed in the United States of America

First Edition, 2017

ISBN:10-0997898631
978-0-9978986-3-7

Cover design and layout by Howell Printing

Howell Printing
345 Barnwell Ave., NW
Aiken, SC 29801
(803) 6489-2545

www.howellprinting.net

# DEDICATION

I dedicate this book to all those students who questioned why other teachers didn't teach the way I did then challenged me to share my methods.

# Transforming Teaching Strategies

## *Ensuring the Success of Kids These Days*

Why is it that some teachers have the best behaved students every school year and others always have to deal with major discipline issues regardless of the subject matter they teach or even the grade level of their class? Why is it that some teachers can challenge their students to achieve beyond the expected standards with astonishing results and other teachers deal with defiant students who resist them every step of the way? Why is it that some teachers always seem to be caught up on school work and others have an ever increasing stack of papers to grade, websites to update and e-mails to respond to? Why is it that some teachers are energized by their students and others are drained and exhausted before day's end?

I have had the good fortune of teaching students ranging from the 7th through 12th grade throughout my 40 plus years in the public school system. Teaching math classes with skill levels from simple mathematics to pre-calculus and everything in between certainly brought about a wide variety of issues. Mistakes were made throughout the years. As I gained experience and new techniques were tried, along with a promise to myself that every new year would be better than the last, changes started to occur. I began to discover the things that were truly important for a positive, enjoyable, stress free learning environment for myself as well as for every single student.

I am more confident than ever that if these strategies are implemented, you will be on a course to experience your best teaching year ever!

First and foremost, we teach kids! Next, we teach subject matter. A student from a journalism class came to me during my instructional planning period and asked to interview me for an article in our school newspaper. Her first question was, "Why do you like teaching math so much?" She was shocked by my response. "I don't like teaching math." She replied, "Then why have you taught it for so long?" I shared with her that I love teaching students; I just use math as a vehicle to do that. She was confused by my response, as perhaps maybe you are. So, let's begin.

I am not qualified to assist you in the teaching of your subject area – unless it is math. However, I am highly qualified in sharing with you strategies in teaching your students. Many of these ideas did not originate with me. Nor did they come from an educational textbook. I have been privileged to teach alongside some pretty amazing teachers from whom I have absorbed some great knowledge which I then implemented in my own classes. I chose to use these strategies and now share them with you. The following solutions to a successful school year are not in any certain order of importance. I simply numbered them so there would be an easy way to reference them. However, I am unwavering in my belief that each is very important and the quicker you can implement them, the faster you can begin enjoying your best year ever.

~ ~ ~ ~ ~ ~ ~ ~ ~ ~ ~ ~ ~ ~ ~ ~ ~ ~ ~ ~ ~ ~ ~ ~ ~ ~ ~ ~ ~ ~ ~ ~

*Additional space has been provided following each strategy to allow you the opportunity to begin brainstorming your own ideas for changes that you may want to begin to implement. This guidebook is also meant to be a **workbook.** ☺

# CONTENTS

# STRATEGY 1
## Let Your Students Know That You Care about Them

It was on my very last day of teaching, prior to retiring, that a young man, whom I had taught Geometry the previous year, came to my room and dropped off a self-made card for me. He quickly left before I had an opportunity to do anything other than greet him. Curiously, I opened the card and began reading. The contents of this simple note touched my heart deeply.

> **Dear Mrs. Mary Thomas,**
> **You may not remember me, I was in your 5th period class last year.**
> **I just want you to know that you really inspired me a lot. I was actually going through a tough time back then and when you did your inspirational speech and showed your daily "thoughts for the day", I actually cried, because it really helped me and made me feel like the world is not such a bad place. I hope you are still doing that kind of helpful thing. You are a good teacher, I'm glad that I met you!!!**
>
> **...They told me I'm not good enough. People made fun of me because I don't speak English very well.  When we always see each other, you always ask me, how are you and say hello to me, to be honest, you are the only person who asked me that in this school. Thank you for that. Your words and your smile really helped me.**
> **Thank you.**

The students need to know that you truly care about them personally. In the message above, the young man didn't express thanks for having learned to find the volume of a sphere, even though he did, and that was one of the many mandated state standards for that curriculum.  He did not express thanks for attaining a B in the class, which he did.  No, in his simple message he chose to express thanks for having been given hope for the future and then being recognized as an individual knowing that someone cared about him long after he had completed the class.

This may seem like an overused cliché, but it is so important... your students don't care how much you know, until they know how much you care. Once they know how much you care about them - you can teach them anything!

# My strategies for change:

# STRATEGY 2
## Choose to Have a Good Day Every Day

Did you know that you can have a good day every single day? Yes, it is your choice. You are the only one who gets to decide how you are going to respond to the many things that you will encounter each day. I recall, decades ago, I went to a motivational convention with many family members. This event extended from Friday evening until Sunday afternoon. We listened to numerous speakers and attended many of the small group breakout sessions. On the drive home I remember feeling a bit overwhelmed with all the amazing information I received and still trying to process it all. However, as time passed, like most information, it became stored in that part of my brain that I have seemingly lost the key. Everything except for one powerful thought.

The speaker asked for all those who were having a good day to stand up. Of course, everyone jumped to their feet. After all, this was a motivational conference. You did not want to be the only one sitting. The speaker continued, of course today is a good day, but if you believe that you can have a good day throughout the entire weekend, remain standing. While most remained standing, he continued once again with a challenge. If you think you can have a good day every day next week continue standing. As he proceeded, those standing diminished in number. He persistently went on until finally he said, remain standing if you believe that you can have a good day every day for the rest of your life. At this point the entire audience was seated; who would dare be so bold as to continue standing for that challenge? Then the speaker stated, and I'll never forget, "To whom did you just give that power to? Who is it that you are going to allow to dictate how you feel on any given day?" I never really thought about it that way before; but from that day on, it was never the same. I discovered an amazing sense of empowerment over my life.

When you have a good day, everyone around you feels better. It will certainly have a positive impact on your students. So, I challenge you to choose to have a good day every day!!

# My strategies for change:

# STRATEGY 3
## Time Management

Be careful about wasting time socializing with peers, searching the web, playing video games or browsing on social media. I'm not saying, don't do it, but be cognizant of the time you spend doing this. If you can't keep up with grading papers, tutoring, doing lesson plans, responding to work emails, maintaining your website, contacting parents, etc. you need to discover a way to find the time for the important work-related tasks. The previously mentioned activities are typically the greatest thieves of our time.

You may want to consider setting the timer on your phone. Make a daily schedule of the amount of time you will allow yourself to spend on these types of entertainment. Tweak this schedule as needed. When that timer goes off, make yourself stop whatever you are doing. Otherwise, it serves no purpose to have a schedule. It may be very difficult at first, but you will be proud of this new disciplined behavior and the much needed tasks you were able to accomplish.

As a society, we waste so many things. It never seems to be that big of a deal. We waste gas driving across town to get a special burger; then we waste food because we super-sized it and cannot eat it all; we waste water brushing our teeth; we waste money buying things we never use or perhaps never wear; we waste electricity leaving the lights on... You get the idea. This is not a problem because we can always acquire more of what we wasted. That is, everything except time. When we waste time, it is gone forever. Never an opportunity to go back, or recycle, or recreate the moment, or buy more time for any given day. Twenty-four hours a day is all any of us get. Be disciplined in using your time wisely. It will allow you to complete your school related tasks more efficiently and timely which is a major stress reliever.

# My strategies for change:

# STRATEGY 4
## Grading Papers

Do yourself and your students a huge favor by grading everything within a 24-hour time period. You will have to use your time wisely and efficiently to accomplish this. It is so tempting to sit back and relax and chat with peers during lunch or perhaps during your instructional planning period. It is important to socialize, collaborate on lessons, and exchange ideas; but if that is minimized, it will allow you to stay on top of your grading and other job related tasks.

It is imperative as you proceed with the next lesson to know the level of comprehension that the students have thus far. It is important to you and them. It makes no sense to give students a quiz if you do not grade it until after the test, which is usually a week later. Too often a student will continue to make the same mistake over and over again not realizing his error because it has not been brought to your or his attention. Graded assessments are important learning tools as you delve into new lessons. Another huge benefit is that your evenings are free to spend as you wish and no more Sunday afternoon school blues, dreading the stack of ungraded papers that you have put off all week. Make every effort to take care of all your school work at school, so you can enjoy your evenings and weekends.

## My strategies for change:

# STRATEGY 5
## Homework Policy

Homework policies have certainly evolved throughout the years; some schools, cities, and even entire countries are making major transformations on this topic. Some are actually eliminating homework; in fact they go so far as to say that they are banning homework. For some teachers there will be no choice in the homework policy, but if given the chance exploring the 'No Homework Policy' could have very favorable outcomes for you and your students.

On the first day of school when classroom procedures are discussed with students, they are presented with the following challenge. Would you be willing to come into class everyday and work from bell to bell (their eyes begin to roll) IF there is no homework assignment? Their immediate response is a resounding YES! They are told that the lessons have been designed to incorporate all that needs to be done within the class period if they are serious about the "bell-to-bell" plan. Naturally they are totally onboard.

This tends to add a new level of intensity to the lessons, more students are engaged, and when given practice worksheets to do, all students are actively participating. Students are taught that there are three steps involved in learning something new. **Watch** how to do the lesson being taught; **attempt** to do the lesson; **teach** someone else how to do the lesson. This has proven to be a wonderful teaching strategy for the students, from the low level class to pre-calculus students. With this technique, students get the help they need immediately from the teacher or students around them. It also creates a wonderful respect and rapport with their classmates.

Think about the countless homework scenarios you typically encounter. Many students will not do the homework for various (and often legitimate) reasons. They were honest in the fact that they told you they didn't do it, and they receive a 0%. Multiple students turned in a completed homework assignment, but they cheated by having their parents do it or perhaps copying from a friend, and they receive a 100%. Some students try to do the homework, but they find it too difficult and have no one to tutor them. It is problematic to give too much credibility to assignments done outside of the classroom. In addition, this will be one more thing YOU don't have to grade!

There are many questions being asked (mostly by students) where and when the idea of homework even originated. Many studies show that homework has no measurable effect on students' learning. Students, on average, spend seven hours a day sitting in classrooms. It seems as though that should be ample time to teach them what they need to learn. No one (teachers and parents included) wants to go home with more school work to do. Perhaps the time could be much better spent with family. Parents could spend more enjoyable time with their children in the evening rather than the constant battle with homework. I recently read an alarming statistic from the Family Research Council that the average dad spends 8 minutes a day in direct conversation with his kids. Perhaps this could be a small catalyst to begin making some important changes.

## My strategies for change:

# STRATEGY 6
## Ticket in the Door

This is directly related to #5. On average, a couple of times each week the students will be given a little open note mini quiz, often referred to as a "ticket in the door." It is normally just 3-4 questions that are directly related to what was taught the day before. Students use their previous day's notes to see if they are able to answer the given questions with a 5-minute time restriction. Leniency is usually granted in the grading of these assessments because the students have just learned the skill, but they still need to be held responsible for what was taught the day prior. This procedure encourages the students to be attentive in class, take good notes, and have the worksheet completed because it will have valuable information for what is on the mini quiz. Students are not allowed to share notes during the quiz; however, they are encouraged to share with someone who was absent after this quiz is completed. A student who was absent the previous day can look at this assessment and see what was taught. These quizzes are easy to grade and must be returned to the student the following day, or they are pretty useless because they guide the lesson for the next day. The teacher will instantly know if there is a need to reteach or move forward. Immediately it is known if a particular student is having trouble, or a simple misunderstanding of a concept can be caught before it becomes a habit. These papers are on the students' desk as they enter the room the following day. Students are always quick to look at theirs, compare with others, and help each other with mistakes. Most of this takes place before it is time to begin a new lesson. Whenever the majority of the class misses the same problem, it will be retaught before moving on. If your school district requires homework grades, this could certainly suffice. All the while, you will have a much better picture of the learning taking place in your classroom.

# My strategies for change:

# STRATEGY 7
## Grading Policy

There are numerous ideas being discussed about grading policies throughout the country. As always we see extremes where some suggest that we eliminate grades totally, others suggest a simple pass/fail policy, and many want to leave it alone because that's the way we have always done it. A Google search lead to additional information where I learned that some school districts use the bell curve, and others used grade scales anywhere from a 6% grade scale to a 20% scale used in Canada. There are other countries which use a numbering system 5 - 1 which would equate to Canada's 20% grade scale.

Most people are in agreement that there is a need for grades and stress the importance of achievement. This is understandable. However, so many school districts (all that I have taught in) have anything below 70% as failing. Every letter grade had, at the most, 10 percentage points separating consecutive letter grades. That is, except the F. If a student gets a 0% on most any assessment, he is doomed for failure. Now this struggling student has to find a way to compensate for a 70% deficit before he is even passing. That would be extremely difficult even for an above average student. This is not a suggestion that every student should pass just because they show up, or they try even though we seem to be living in a world where everyone on the team gets a trophy. However, it doesn't take a math teacher to see that it becomes nearly impossible for a student to recover from such a deficit; and as soon as they realize it, they are going to quit trying. This strategy is not about giving low achievers trophies; it is more about doing everything possible to keep them in the game.

As a teacher, you don't have the ability to change the grading policy of a school district; in fact, in most school districts the grading system that is used is programed into the computer where your grades are to be inputted, and the computer does the rest. Nevertheless, you do have the freedom to change your bottom line. If a student doesn't take a test, a 0% is recorded. This just reminds you, as well as the student, a test needs to be made up. However, if a student makes an honest effort on a test and comes up terribly short of passing, you can determine the lowest grade you will give. My bottom line was a 50%. There are some school districts, who have recognized the problem with this policy and have adopted the same practice of 50% being the bottom line as well.

This 50% is still a failing grade. It is a 20% deficit from passing. However, it is much more realistic for a student to recover. If the student continues in this pattern, thinking he can get a 50% with little or no effort, he is still failing. You initially didn't really give him anything other than an opportunity or perhaps some hope. If he continues to be happy with just a 50% rather than a 0% he will still fail, but it was he, who took himself out of the game.

## My strategies for change:

# STRATEGY 8
## Rewards

There is a large Tupperware container that I keep filled with snack-size candy bars, Skittles, and Starbursts in one of the drawers of a file cabinet in my classroom. It is close to my desk so I can monitor it. I am not concerned with my students getting into the candy box, they know better. It's my teacher friends that I have to keep an eye on. The contents of this box contain the rewards that are offered for various accomplishments. Students who get an A on a test will be recipients of a treat. Students are invited to come to my desk and help themselves to their delight, as their name and grade are announced to the class. I believe it is important to celebrate their success. Sometimes if a struggling student finally makes a C, he is quietly invited to stay after class and is allowed to partake in selecting something from the candy bar box. If a student catches me in a mistake (which happens more often than I would like to admit) when doing problems on the board, that's a trip to the candy bar box. This practice helps keep students attentive looking for something wrong – everyone wins. If a student answers or even asks a challenging question, it gives him an opportunity for candy. What is remarkable is that before long, many of the students like the positive accolades more than the candy and soon will not even stay after class for the sweet reward. The candy was simply bait used to catch the big fish – achieving the ultimate goal of attentive self-motivated students who take pride in their accomplishments. The positive reinforcement and continuous praises work wonders in keeping students motivated.

FYI... when contemplating rewards - even high school students like stickers on their papers.

# My strategies for change:

# STRATEGY 9
## No Questions Go Unanswered

When discussing new or even previously taught material, or reviewing for an assessment, Q & A (question/answer) style teaching rather than simply lecturing is often used. An answer is expected for every teacher-generated question. Do not allow this process to continue if no one answers the question. This teaching tactic breaks down if the students are not engaged. The effectiveness of this teaching style is dependent on student involvement. If the class is sitting back waiting for you to answer the question you asked, you are right back to lecturing. If the entire class seems stumped by a question, I'll give them the answer and then ask the question again. Now many students, with a grin, will answer, but they know I expect feedback. This will allow for more engaging Q & A as we continue. Students know to be attentive and ready to answer if called upon individually. Be careful that one student does not dominate this process; that is the same as you answering all the questions.

Now there is a flip side to this strategy. You must answer the students' questions. You would be surprised at the number of kids whom would come to me asking for assistance with their math homework or test reviews, whom I did not know. Their friends, who were my (past or current) students told them I would tutor them. While working with these students, I would ask them why they did not seek assistance with their own teacher, and I was quite disheartened by many responses. They said things like, "Every time I raise my hand she rolls her eyes." "She screamed at me for not paying attention." "She embarrasses the students when they ask questions." "She makes me feel stupid, when I ask a question." "She told me that I should've learned that last year, and she doesn't have time to teach it now." Teachers, whether this is actually true or not does not matter. This is the students' perception, so it is indeed their reality.

It has been said that, "There is no such thing as a stupid question." As teachers, we will quickly debate that! But, with that being said, asking questions is an important part of the learning process, whether teacher or student-generated. The dialog is a powerful instructional tool.

I promise that I understand the need for moving on and the stress that you are under to stay on schedule in an attempt to complete all the state mandated standards. It is easy to get frustrated with students and answering the same questions over and over, but don't always assume that they were inattentive. Often times, they need to see or hear the lesson more than once to comprehend it. How many times did it take your students to teach you how to tweet?

Give credibility to the question, and answer it. If they care enough and in some cases, brave enough to ask the question you should be patient enough to answer it. The Q &A time during class is a huge part of the learning process; don't allow this communication to break down because your students are afraid of how you may react to their question. In fact, you should never react! If the question seems outrageous, take a deep breath, gather your thoughts, and then respond to their question.

Most students were comfortable with this teaching style because they knew they could trust me not to embarrass them. This can only be an effective teaching strategy if students knew your expectations and feel comfortable in your class. It is you, as the teacher, who controls both of these important aspects.

## My strategies for change:

# STRATEGY 10
## No Wrong Answers

When teaching, especially the lower level students, nothing will shut them down quicker than telling them publicly, in front of their peers, that they are wrong. I know, as well as you, that we typically get far more wrong answers than correct ones, especially when we are tossing out new ideas and we want students to engage in the thought process of exploring new concepts. Some students are far more vulnerable to the humiliation of being wrong than others. You know them, they won't even lift their heads to look at you for fear you will call on them. Well, call on them anyway. Feed them enough information and guide them to a conclusion that they thought was their own and then feel so proud because you celebrated their answer and offer them a trip to the candy bar box. On other occasions, if a student answers wrongly, it is imperative to find something positive to say in your response. "You know, I can see why you would say that." Or, "That's how we are going to do the problems in the next section; I think you were looking ahead." Or, "You would be exactly right if we were talking about *this* rather than *that*." Always find something positive to say and then guide them to the correct way to solve the problem. Allow them to feel empowered even in their mistake. You do not ever want them to shut down, feel stupid, or feel that they will never understand the lesson being taught. Even when grading their papers, highlight what is right, and assure them that you can help them fix what is wrong.

## My strategies for change:

# STRATEGY 11
## Thought for the Day

This was probably one of the best things that was ever implemented in my daily lesson plans. The Thought for the Day! (TFTD). A file folder was created with nearly 300 TFTD. Some are silly and fun. Some are patriotic for special holidays. Most of them are thought-provoking, motivational statements that cause the students to think beyond today, and more importantly, beyond themselves. As the students enter the room, typically the lights are turned off, and the TFTD is displayed on the smart board. The students take their seats and settle in for class. Prior to beginning the lesson, the TFTD is addressed. Initially, the quote was merely read, and then the lesson would begin. Interestingly, before long, the students asked what the TFTD meant to me; they were searching for a deeper meaning than just reading words. I was always eager to share with them and a little surprised that they were so interested. Because of their interest, I began telling stories relating the motivating quotes to something personal that I had dealt with or perhaps a struggle of an unnamed student. Then the ideas were extended far beyond the classroom to worldwide issues, opening their eyes to roles as citizens rather than students. When I shared these TFTD with my students, they were so attentive, I would think to myself, "I wish they were this attentive when I was teaching the math lesson." It excited me when students would e-mail TFTDs that they had found and asked if I would share them. Through this daily routine, the students realized that I cared about them. They quickly appreciated that their personal growth, growth into adulthood, was more important to me than the math class because in my lesson plans TFTD always came first. (This is evident by the young man's card in #1.) However, this just opened the door for me to be able to teach them anything! Even math!

# My strategies for change:

# STRATEGY 12
## Have Fun

Somewhere along the line someone told teachers that they shouldn't smile at their students until Christmas. This idea has been around a long time, because I heard this when I first began teaching insinuating that there should be no interaction with students other than the lesson. We should promote strict guidelines and let them know who is in charge. If I were texting my response to this old adage, it would be...OMG! SMH!

Do not misunderstand me. I am a strong believer in order and discipline. I believe that there should be structure with well-known boundaries. Respect for authority is imperative because without it, everything will collapse. However, I also believe there is a more powerful and more effective way to produce these important outcomes.

We should be developing relationships not trying to avoid them. At the beginning of the school year, you should smile and smile a lot. Your body language speaks louder than words. Your smile says, "I'm glad you're here." It gives a glimmer of your passion. It lets them know that you are a happy person. They quickly get a sense that they are going to enjoy your class. It also sets a tone of how they will be treated as well as how they should treat others. You will not need to tell them how to act; your smile will dictate that.

I want to take this one step further. It is important to laugh with your students. That's right! You need to laugh. I recently read the powerful effects that laughter has on your body. It is better than any prescription medicine. We have all heard the quote that laughter is the best medicine, and here are just a few reasons why.

Laughter can lower your blood pressure which can reduce the risk of stroke and heart attack. Laughter reduces stress hormones which reduces anxiety and stress. Laughter has a calming effect and helps people sleep better. It boosts your immune system by activating the T-cells which are specialized immune system cells that immediately begin to help fight off sickness. Laughter releases endorphins which are the body's natural pain killers. They will reduce chronic pain and help you feel good all over. This also helps people who suffer from depression.

OK teachers this is one of the best reasons to encourage laughter in the classroom; it triggers brain activity, specifically the right side of the brain which increases creative thinking and decision-making skills. In addition, it is absolutely FREE with no negative side effects.

I'm not suggesting that you turn your classroom into a comedy act. I'm simply saying that we should have a sense of humor. Tell your students a joke or a funny story about a historical figure that you are studying. Perhaps even a funny story about yourself or something you heard on the news. Did you know that children on average laugh 200 times a day while adults laugh 4 times a day? As adults, we tend to take ourselves way too seriously. In addition, I'm not suggesting that you compromise order and discipline within your classroom. No, just add humor. Have fun! Not only will you find far more enjoyment in your class but so will your students. Perhaps, tonight, instead of grading papers, relax with family or friends and watch a comedy on Netflix.

## My strategies for change:

# STRATEGY 13
## Learn Your Students' Names

Nothing makes you feel as special and that you belong to a group quite as much as someone calling you by name.  Most schools have the data and technology which will allow you to print out a seating chart with the students' pictures along with their name. You can cheat and have that seating chart in your hand along with your lessons. Your students will be pleasantly surprised when you call them by name. In addition, those students who might be potential problems will not be so quick to show out if you already call them by name.

I attend a very large church with over 1800 families in the parish. It always warms my heart when the priest greets me by name after the service. I know first hand how difficult it is to remember so many names, and he knows mine. Yes, it makes me feel special.  That is exactly why every effort is made to learn names quickly.

It is also important to encourage your students to learn each others' names. So early on, plan activities that require group interaction which gives them the opportunity to learn others' names. It will give everyone a sense of being on the same team; a sense of belonging; a feeling of importance.

## My strategies for change:

# STRATEGY 14
## Disciplining Students

Even the very best of teaching strategies will not eliminate every discipline issue. You will have minor discipline issues such as students sleeping in your class; students with attendance issues; students coming to class unprepared; students out of their seats while you are teaching; and students violating the dress code. You will possibly have a major issue such as students arguing or perhaps even fighting; student verbally disrespecting you; cheating...

The possible disruptions that could occur in your classroom are innumerable. They can certainly be minimized by using effective teaching strategies, but I can promise you that "stuff" happens, and it will happen in your class sooner or later.

Do not take it personally, even if the verbal attack is against you. Do not **react** to the situation. Take a moment, take a deep breath, take yourself out of the equation (that's my math mind), and then **respond**. Obviously, it depends on the severity of the action, but typically, ask the student to stick around after class for a minute. In most cases, the student will be on his best behavior the remainder of the class, hoping you will forget about it. If they challenge you, demanding to know *why?*; simply respond that it will be discussed after class. It is important to get all the students back on track as quickly as possible, and do not allow other students to even address the issue. This also gives both you and the perpetrator an opportunity to assess the situation before actually dealing with it. It allows you the chance, as well, to display to the entire class that the behavior was not acceptable and will be dealt with.

Do not argue, verbally accuse, or reprimand students in front of their peers. Too often this will add fuel to an already heated issue that will become escalated to a point where you lose total control or perhaps respect of the entire class. You will, too quickly, be engaged in a situation where no one wins. On the other hand, asking a student to stay behind a moment will allow you an opportunity to build a relationship with this person rather than alienate them. You will often be surprised by their side of the story. The mere fact that you cared enough to ask, rather than verbally reprimand, can have amazing results for everyone involved.

# My strategies for change:

# STRATEGY 15
## Be Cautious of Others' Opinions about Your Students

Be leery of teachers wanting to see your class roster when school begins. Rarely is it productive. So often other teachers will fill your head with horror stories of past students. Occasionally, it might be helpful to have a heads up for potential problems, but typically the guidance counselor will see you about those situations. Just because someone was disruptive or did not preform well in one teacher's class, do not write them off for your class. It's just not fair to judge their past performances from a previous teacher. It could have been a personality conflict with a past teacher. Give them a chance! Students mature and change from year to year (sometimes day to day). Do not hold past performances against them. That's why it is better if you were not even aware of former mischievousness. Allow them to start with a clean slate and just possibly, you are the person that can bring real change in a troubled student's life. Besides, you have something to offer your students that no one in past could – You have YOU!

## My strategies for change:

# STRATEGY 16
## Meet Students at the Door

Whenever possible, greet your students at the door. Realize that sometimes you will be tied up (Whoa! I hope not *physically* tied up) in your room, finishing with one class and getting ready to begin the next. Note too, that sooner or later, a restroom call will take top priority. However, the idea is, rather than congregating with teachers in the hall, welcome your students into your classroom. This gives you a chance to acknowledge them individually and invites an opportunity for any one-on-one discussion which might be desired by you or the student. When the student feels welcomed, it quickly sets the mood for a positive learning environment. One of the highest compliments that a student could give you is to state that they really enjoy coming to your class. Begin striving for that goal. Start by saying hello.

## My strategies for change:

# STRATEGY 17
## Beware of the Teachers' Lounge

It is typically a place to relax, get out of your classroom for a break, and possibly catch a snack. Often teachers will eat their lunch in this lounge. Keep your break to a minimum. Before you know it, you have squandered all your free time with nothing to show for it. Stay focused, remind yourself that you would much prefer any free time spent relaxing at home in the evening.

As teachers begin to gather in the lounge the conversation inevitably turns towards their one commonality - kids! All too often this time is used to vent! Usually, the venting is student related, but other teachers and the administration are also fair game. If you find the air of constant negativity surrounding you in this place - get out! Attitudes, whether positive or negative, are contagious. This undesirable attitude will physically drain you of your energy, but in contrast a positive attitude will energize you. Usually one person will find it nearly impossible to change the environment of the lounge. However, any person is free to escape from that environment if they choose.

## My strategies for change:

# STRATEGY 18
## Teach with Passion

If you are not passionate about who you teach, what you teach, and how you teach, you will never reach your students. They will emulate your excitement or apparent boredom. Teach deeper than the lesson. Tell stories. When talking about Thomas Edison, for example, don't just mention he invented the light bulb. Tell them 1,000 times he tried and was unsuccessful, but he never gave up. Tell them the story that he was expelled from elementary school because his teachers told his mother he was too stupid to learn. However, his mom told him he couldn't go to school because he was too smart, and they didn't have teachers qualified to teach him. He believed her and became the greatest inventor of the century. Your students will never forget Thomas Edison or the life lessons of never giving up or the importance of believing in yourself. Share personal stories that might relate to a lesson. Make your lesson applicable.

This may take a little research, but just ask Siri or Google, they know everything, and you will have stories to share year after year. Tell them stories. Make it exciting. Be passionate.

## My strategies for change:

# STRATEGY 19
## Have Your Best School Year Ever

The brain is a powerful complex organ that actually believes EVERYTHING that you tell it. Did you know that under hypnosis, when the conscious mind is quiet and the subconscious mind is attentive, a hypnotist can convince you that a pencil is a hot match? Not only that, if he touches the pencil to your skin, it will actually cause your skin to blister. So, how about using that amazing resource to ensure your success this year. Every morning tell yourself that this is your best school year. Then when you get to school, tell others that this is your best school year ever. Tell your students that, and they will take pride in that statement. Tell each of your classes that they are your favorite class. In the evening, when you begin drifting off to sleep continually tell yourself, "I love my job!"

There was a veteran teacher who was new to our school, and early in the school year she shared with me that her last class of the day was horrible; they were definitely her worst class of the day. I responded that they will continue to be bad. She questioned my response, "Why do you think that?" I said, "Because you do, and you have already told them they were the worst." She quickly asked, "What should I do?" "Next week, begin telling them that you see a major improvement in their behavior. Tell them how much more enjoyable it is seeing them come into class. Before long, tell them that they are quickly becoming your favorite class. Finally tell them, they are by far your best class ever and how much you look forward to ending your day with them." Several months later, she popped into my room and said, "I've been meaning to tell you that your idea worked." Confused, I asked her what she was referring to. She reminded me of my suggestion from earlier and said, "This truly is my favorite class. I really enjoy them now and I can actually teach the lesson and even though it is the end of the day they are still attentive and respectful." My response - "I'm not surprised!" ☺

You can label them your *Class from Hell* or your *Best Class Ever* - either way you will be correct. Which would you prefer?

# My strategies for change:

# CONCLUSION

In compiling these strategies, I was unaware of actually how many there were until I numbered them as I was typing. If you are uncomfortable (perhaps a little OCD) with the fact that there are nineteen listed strategies, I would like to invite you to write your own #20 strategy that has brought success in your classroom. Keep it positive and then share your ideas with others on my website.

Think of this guidebook as a toolbox. Some of these tools might be very familiar to you and others quite foreign. Perhaps you are an old pro with some, and possibly, it was you who shared the strategy with me. As you begin to delve into unfamiliar territory, feel free to move slowly and implement new practices as you see fit. Do not feel like you have to wait for a new school year or even a new semester to begin making changes. We are always challenging our students to grow and make changes as needed; they will appreciate seeing that quality in you, as their teacher. Simply relate to them that you believe that you have an idea that will work better in a particular situation, such as homework, grading, thoughts for the day... any one of the above strategies. Simply move at the pace you are most comfortable, but always move forward.

This teacher guidebook was not written so that you will teach *The Mary Thomas Method*, because in reality, there is no such thing. I promised myself to tweak my teaching methods every semester collecting new ideas and using a culmination of years of strategies that I have developed or learned from others, taking on the responsibility in continuing to attempt to become the best version of me, because my students deserved no less. My goal in writing this guidebook is to share strategies that work, which will guide you in developing your own teaching method that will begin to unlock the best version of **you**. Your students deserve no less.

**website:** www.marythomassolutions.com
**email:** marythomassolutions1@gmail.com
*additional copies of this book may be purchased on the above website*

MARY THOMAS
SOLUT!ONS
TRANSFORMING TEACHING STRATEGIES

# My strategies for change:

# My strategies for change:

# Testimonies

If you are a veteran teacher who has lost your spark for this profession or if you are just beginning your teaching career and nervous about the reality of actually having your own students for the first time, Mary Thomas has identified a formula that any teacher, of any curriculum, on any grade level, can follow to achieve outstanding results. A formula that will help you unlock your full potential.

-William A. Gallman, Ph.D, Psychologist (retired)
Deputy Superintendent: Aiken Co Public Schools, SC


In this guidebook, Mary Thomas shares her forty-three years of teaching strategies in which she has honed to perfection. This book is a virtual toolbox filled with empowering tactics that will change or perhaps fine tune teaching techniques that will bring about unbelievable results for you as well as your students.

-Della Hughes, Ed.S.
Graduation Coach, Columbia Co, GA


Mary Thomas' guidebook offers powerful, positive, and practical strategies for designing a dynamic environment for classroom instruction. She shares proven techniques that will create an atmosphere in which students are not only engaged but enjoy the lessons being taught. Her ideas, when implemented, establishes a comfortable and safe learning environment that students engage in with pride and enthusiasm.

-John Nix, M. Ed.
Asst. Principal, Lexington School District 1, SC

# ABOUT THE AUTHOR

Mary Thomas started her teaching career in Charleston, WV where she was born, raised and graduated college. A few years later she went back to school and received her Master's degree from Marshall University. Mary taught and coached for 11 years in Charleston before moving to Aiken, SC where she taught for an additional 24 years. After retiring in SC she went to Evans GA where she taught an additional 8 years.

Mary has recently retired from teaching mathematics after 43 years in the classroom of middle and high schools. She was very involved with students outside the classroom as well as through coaching and club advisory roles. Mary has been the recipient of numerous awards for her high achievements as a teacher, coach, club advisor, as well as an active leader in community service projects. Among the many top awards she has received she states that she is proudest of her county's "Woman of the Year Award" because it is given due to the accumulation of the many previous awards.

Mary is an Amazon #1 best selling author of the popular motivational book, *Kids These Days* which details the true events of many of her incredible students who overcame tremendous odds to achieve their goals. In addition to teaching and writing, she is a highly sought after motivational speaker to audiences of teachers as well as teens.

Mary and her husband Joe reside in Aiken, SC, and their daughter Christina is an RN at MUSC in Charleston, SC.